Pebble® Plus

Meet **Desert** ANIMALS

CAMELS

by Rose Davin

raintree

a Capstone company — publishers for children

Raintree is an imprint of Capstone Global Library Limited, a company incorporated in England and Wales having its registered office at 264 Banbury Road, Oxford, OX2 7DY – Registered company number: 6695582

www.raintree.co.uk
myorders@raintree.co.uk

ISBN 978 1 4747 3656 5 (hardback)
20 19 18 17 16
10 9 8 7 6 5 4 3 2 1

ISBN 978 1 4747 3662 6 (paperback)
21 20 19 18 17
10 9 8 7 6 5 4 3 2 1

British Library Cataloguing in Publication Data
A full catalogue record for this book is available from the British Library.

Editorial Credits
Marysa Storm and Alesha Sullivan, editors; Kayla Rossow, designer; Ruth Smith, media researcher; Kathy McColley, production specialist

Photo Credits
Capstone Press: 6; Dreamstime: © Aleksandr Frolov, 21; Shutterstock: Asian Images, 2, 24, David Steele, 19, Don Mammoser, 17, Gillian Holliday, cover, back cover, Hitdelight, 24, Maxim Petrichuk, 9 muznabutt, 7, Naiyyer, 11, Olena Tur, 5, optionm, 22, schankz, 13, Wolfgang Zwanzger, 1, YANGCHAO, 15

Note to Parents and Teachers

The Meet Desert Animals set supports national curriculum standards for science related to life science and ecosystems. This book describes and illustrates camels. The images support early readers in understanding the text. The repetition of words and phrases helps early readers learn new words. This book also introduces early readers to subject-specific vocabulary words, which are defined in the Glossary section. Early readers may need assistance to read some words and to use the Table of Contents, Glossary, Read more, Websites, Comprehension questions and Index sections of the book.

Printed and bound in India.

CONTENTS

WOOLY WORKERS

Camels roll in the desert sand.

They nap in the hot sun.

But camels work too. They carry

people and heavy loads.

Most camels live in deserts in Africa and Asia. Camels follow one another across the sand. They stay together in groups called herds.

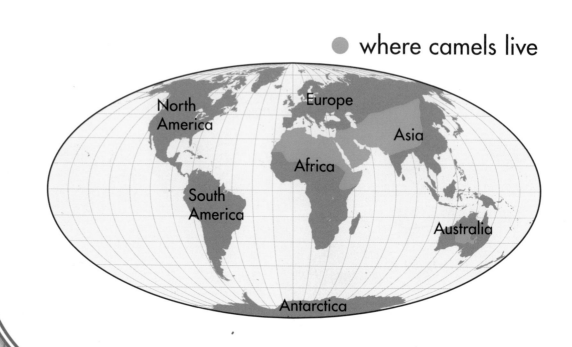

● where camels live

North America

Europe

Asia

Africa

South America

Australia

Antarctica

FROM HEAD TO TOE

Camels have one or two humps.

The humps store fat. Their bodies
use the fat when they can't find food.

Bactrian camel

During sandstorms camels can
close their nostrils. This keeps sand out.
Their long eyelashes keep sand out
of their eyes.

Camels have wide, round feet with pads. Their feet keep them from sinking into the sand. Some camels are almost as fast as horses. They can run 64 kilometres (40 miles) per hour.

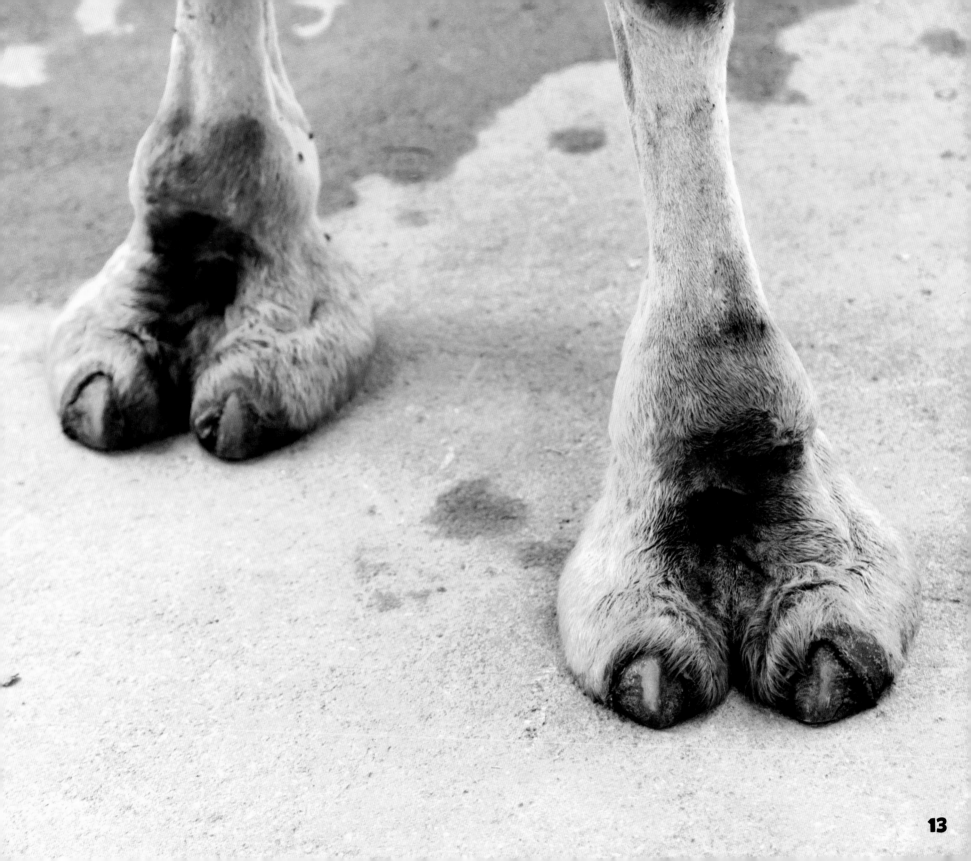

TIME TO EAT

Camels are not picky eaters.

They nibble on any desert

plants they can find. Wild onions

are some of their favourites.

Camels can go for months without water.

Thirsty camels can drink about 100 litres

(30 gallons) of water in 10 minutes.

Slurp!

LIFE CYCLE

Female camels usually have one calf every two years. Calves can walk on the day they are born. They drink their mothers' milk for about one year.

19

Young camels stay with their family

herd for about four years.

Camels can live more than 40 years.

Glossary

calf young camel

desert dry area of land with few plants; deserts receive very little rain

herd large group of animals that lives or moves together

hump raised rounded area on the back of a camel; camel humps are filled with fat

nostril opening in the nose used to breathe and smell

Read more

Baby Camels (Super Cute!), Megan Borgert-Spaniol (Blastoff! Readers, 2016)

Camels (Desert Animals), Leo Statts (Abdo Zoom, 2016)

Deserts (What Animals Live Here?), M.J. Knight (Franklin Watts, 2016)

Websites

http://www.bbc.co.uk/nature/life/Camel
Learn about camels and the way camels live.

http://animals.nationalgeographic.com/animals/mammals/dromedary-camel/
Discover facts, look at photos and watch videos of camels on the National Geographic website.

Comprehension questions

1. Name two parts of the camel's body that help it to live in the desert. Tell how these parts help the camel.

2. Read page 18. Why do you think it's important for calves to stand soon after they are born?

3. Think of another animal that lives in the desert. How is the camel the same or different from that animal?

Index